DESIRE

&

ITS IMPOSSIBILITIES

POEMS OF DISAPPOINTMENT

DESIRE

&

ITS IMPOSSIBILITIES

POEMS OF DISAPPOINTMENT

VANTY

For anyone who has lost themselves
In the depths of love & desire
You will resurface
You will be found

PREFACE

I loved someone more than I loved myself and in the process I slowly disappeared. Parts of me chipped away as time moved forward. I wrote these poems one by one, year by year. I put them away in random places. Some poems in my notes app, some emailed to myself, and some written in my journals. By the end of the relationship, I had amassed poetry that spanned nearly twenty years.

It's rare and beautiful to love someone who can turn your emotions inside out. It's also devastating to let yourself be turned inside out.

The five chapters developed naturally as I began to put the book together. These are not the stages of grief but the stages of a love affair.

The love for another and the love for myself.

I found solace in nature and the night sky. Symbolism of the moon and sea weave together throughout the book. In the end an allegorical poetic story about Desire, Devotion, Disappointment, Devastation, and Destiny.

Contents

DESIRE

ETERNAL FLAME

Desire

Through the passage of time

I will find you

In every lifetime

In every timeline

You are the magic

I search for

With every gust of wind

I feel you there

In the ache of my heart

I hear you whisper my name

FLOWER

In the night

When the air is dark

And your breath is tight

The sky black

Under no moon

I am your flower

Where you stand

No wind blows

The air is still and your eyes closed

Longing for summer

I am your flower

When the heart breaks

There comes the light

The ground cracks

And water finds its path

There is nothing

But space and wrath

When the sky is vast and endless

There

You will find me blooming

At last

In the small crevices of you

I am your flower

HONEY

You

Your love

Are drops of honey in my hair

Sticky, messy

Damaging and nourishing

Drops of milk on my lips

Sweet, delicious

Warm and cold

Dripping. Slowly.

Feels good.

I'm a mess.

I don't like it

But I want more

You

Your love

When the rose bud seek

The warmth of the sun

Vines, thorn filled crawling

Patiently up the back of my neck

Digging itself into my skin, softly

Anchoring, stable

Reaching for the light

Yearning

To blossom

WARMTH

I miss you like summer

In the winter's rain

Drench me in warmth

Fresh light in the morning

Come again

...and again...

THE CURE

You can cure death

With just your lips

One

Drip

of

Divine

Happiness

A GOOD MORNING

I loved looking at him

My neck reaching for his lips

He hovered over me like

The morning fog

My hands reaching for his face

A soft breeze on my fingertips

His presence made me feel safe

His body protected me

Warmed me.

Seduced me.

He was delicious.

I enjoyed taking bites of him

Sweet bites of fruit

He was the honey

Drizzled

On my breakfast nectarines

HUNGER

Deaf, numb, and blind

All I feel is hunger

For you

For a breath

For more

I don't know who I am or what I want

My mind disappears

My body evaporates

I am nothing and everything

All at once

You are Divine

FAMISHED

Do you miss me?

I

AM

STARVING

LONGING

You put your hand under my head

Around my neck

It took me by surprise

Yet, I immediately

Surrendered

Closed my eyes

And let my head fall back

Into your grasp

You kissed my lips with a quick breath

Stole my soul

A deep inhale

I lingered

On your fading lips

As you pulled away

I want you

I want you all the time

SOFT KISS

A kiss

Soft wetness

Let me breathe

A slow inhale

I keep you

SWEET LULLABY

I loved him.

He saw the little me inside my eyes

Wrapped his warmth around her

With one big hug

A safety blanket

His stare lulled my heart to sleep

My breath

His breath

Together like a lullaby

THUNDER

I wanted you

When I didn't even want myself

Thunder was my music

With each heart beat

Cracking like purple skies

The only beauty

I could find

Was in you

Even the evening night

Finds its light

And in you

Beneath your shadows

I found love

STORM

The sky in shades of purple and blue

As the heavens roared

With the aggression of my heart

I have missed you

For the love that once existed

Seemed like a dream

Separated by the planets and stars

I wait for the nights to reappear

Lightening cracks like a whip

And ignites the fire in my heart

Come back to me

MIDNIGHT

I loved you in this world

That was rare and fleeting

When the days are long

The moon full and the wind warm

I loved you drunk late into the night

Where the hours passed without flight

When the wind touches my face

I think of your gentle kiss

The sun returns

A sunrise wish

I remembered I loved you

And that you loved me too

DEVOTION

MOONSTRUCK

If my heart was the ocean

Your breath the moon

Would you pull

And push

My devotion

Away?

HUMID

He's humid

As imposing as a thunderstorm but

Without relief.

Annoying, irritating at any temperature

Clinging to my skin

Unrelenting.

Condensation on windows

His loving

Heavy

Wet

Damp

Inescapable

Like a midsummer's night

SECRET

It is difficult for the mouth

To speak

What the heart is begging

To keep

Secret

DEVOTION

Devotion

Is

Fickle

As

Flowers

Usually

Are

INTRUDER

You are a cancer

I cannot rid

In the depths of

My bones

You

Devour

Me

SURRENDER

Cut me in half

Split me down my meridian

I am done

Come steal my magic

And let my flickering light

Fill you up

Take me to the heavens

And leave my body

To the dirt

I am yours

HOPE

I hope for love

But the pain is comforting too.

I'll take the latter if the first isn't available

In time the latter becomes the first

And love becomes a forgotten dream

I want you to hurt me.

If I can't feel love

I want the pain.

Maybe

There

I will find you.

LIE TO ME

Tell me you love me.

Just once

Even if it's a lie

I want to know how it feels to be her

I can decide for myself if it's true

I want to hear those words

Leave your mouth

Just once

I would stop time if only

You would love me.

Just once

CUTS

Small cuts

Are not

Inconsequential

Large wounds

Don't hurt

They bleed

Why don't you cut

My heart out already?

Punish me

HEART LOCKET

I loved him once

A long time ago

He reached his hand into my chest cavity

Held onto my heart

Locked his fingertips into place

Anchored it to his thoughts

So when he commanded

I would love him

I'd hear his wishes

And obey

RUST

I've gotten so good at feeling

My heart break

You taught me that

Now I can do it to myself

In the absence of

You

It longs for more

My heart breaks itself just to

Remember your face

Your kiss, your stare

Your lips, it's so unfair

What does it matter anyway

You've changed the air

And turned me

Into rust

BROKE ME

I broke my own heart just so you couldn't do it

I broke my own heart just so you couldn't have it

I broke my own heart just so you couldn't love me

I broke my own heart just so you couldn't steal it

I broke my own heart just so you couldn't keep me

I broke my own heart just so I wouldn't give it to

You

I broke my own heart just so I wouldn't feel the

Pain of

Losing

You

I broke my own heart just so I wouldn't break into

Pieces

Again

Because of

You,

I'm

Broken

HAPPINESS

For a moment I smiled at him

With the same smile I give to those

Who have never

Hurt me

For a moment I forgot

He shattered me

I smiled my carefree smile

The smile I give to those

I trust

For a moment

I smiled

With glittering

Happy eyes

Reserved for new lovers

Filled with hope

For a moment

I lost myself

I forgot my place

I smiled at him as though he had

Never caused me

To go insane

COMFORT

I seek comfort from those

Who have hurt me

A warm familiar blanket

Suffocate and smother me

Engulf me

In your disappointing

Embrace

OUT TO SEA

The line between hope and despair

Gently rocks

Back and forth

While quiet desperation

Slowly

Rips me out

To

Sea

DARK LOVE

This love is dark

I'm addicted to its magic

You have stolen my thoughts

Dismantled my heart

Picked it apart

Piece by piece

I've lost my way

I can no longer see my

Fate

You have lead me down

Astray

Your mouth so sweet

I'm tempted to stay

In this

Terrible place

The disappointments

Don't stop coming

Lost in false

Hopes

Disillusioned

Promises

Still

I want to stay

VENOM

Fill me to the brim

Fill in all my cracks

All the broken pieces of me

With your venom

It's better than nothing

It's better than not wanting

Me

At all

DISAPPOINTMENT

EPIPHANY

Remember when you were a little kid

A dreamer

A visionary

A romantic

Believing that love lasted forever

If only

You could just find that person

Your person

Who your soul recognized

With the same goals and traumas as you

Without words

With a glance

You could hear their thoughts

Feel their heart beat

The same as yours

One day

Your heart betrays you

Suddenly

You've changed

Grown

And your guilty eyes

Can't hide

The other you

I'm sorry

Surprise

I never knew

It was possible

To not love the imaginary you

Disappointing isn't it?

After the love falls away

Just one gust

Like a leaf in Autumn

Clinging onto its branch

By a tiny attachment

You realize

It was all a

Lie

STILLNESS

Jazz

My blanket

Wraps around

My heart

Before the stillness

Of the night

Comes

To collect

Its due

SEASONS

I fell in love with the seasons

Knowing they will change

I found comfort in the unpredictability

Certain of its uncertainty

I fell in love with my enemy

Hoping for this change

But they are not the same

Certainty came in waves of disappointment

Unlike contentment in the

Passing of time

It was Hell that came

To never end

I hoped for the familiar feeling

Of wonder and surprise

Instead

I received horror

And my

Demise

PRIDE

You know too late

When a woman withdraws her love

Nothing can prepare you

For her absence

When did she disappear?

You will never know

Tears that do not soothe

The soul

The heart breaks loud

The quietness of loss

Overwhelming

A love gone

Are you proud?

FIREWALL

Every word

A potential spark

To start a fire

Walls so high

Even desire

Can't pass

GLASS

Two broken hearts

Don't become one

Shards that will

Never fit together

No matter how hard

We

Try

PAIN

I've yet to meet

A man

Who loved himself

Enough

To love a woman

Without need for

Cruelty

ARROW

One day my arrow will pierce his heart

Sorrow held will burst the dam

Leaking fear and anguish

Madness

Unfortunate confusion

SILENCE

My tongue alone

In its empty temple

Fails to deliver.

My heart,

Silent,

Signals the end

Of its fight.

TO BE FORGOTTEN

Thinking about

Someone

Who doesn't

Matter

Anymore.

A HAUNTING

I traveled the world

To run from your hurt

I moved to the mountains to

Escape your wretched love

But you convinced them to

Move out of the way for you

I failed to guard the door

You were patient

Apathetic

It made me want you more

I was wrong

Disappointment wins every time

Worse,

I was disappointed in myself.

Every night

The urgency to leave

A consistent reminder

To run faster

Than the memories of you

Can reach

All the corners

Of my mind

SHADOW

My love burns long after its death

Like stars,

The light cuts through the darkness

For eternity

Or a shadow

A smudge in the heavens

Of what was once there

The ash left

After the last light

GHOST

I was in a relationship with a ghost

A figment of my imagination

A saturation of obsession

Uncontrollable possession

A demon unbeknownst to me

Hunting so cleverly

A soulless being who was never there

Who lived in the realms in between air

A mirage

A delusion

An illusion that was so unfair

ROSES

The doorbell rang

Again and again

Roses by the dozens

More and more

Words fewer than the petals

Falling at the door

My forgiveness in exchange

Red, pink, white, and yellow

Flowers overflowing

Lillies, lilacs, love pruned

Just to say hello

Our lust and apologies

Spanned seven thousand three hundred days

It's time to take these flowers

To the grave

DEVASTATION

LAW OF ENTANGLEMENT

When will I retrieve

My self worth?

I see it like the fresh water in a

Deep well

But can't get to it

I know

I deserve myself

All the hidden faces

Of a broken crystal

I can't get rid of these pieces

That have embedded themselves

Into my skin

I don't know where the value ends

And my undeserving self

Begins

They're entangled together

Energetically bounded

Like a sticky veil

Lace I want to pull off my face

On my wedding day

Reveal the parts behind this

Heavy looming door

An intricately carved 8th century panel

Gold plated, rubies and emerald chunks

Sharp to the touch

Two photons flying through the air

Sharp shooter bullets into my eyes

Speeding and lighting up through my body

Electric

Out the tips of my pointer fingers

Separate but together

Worth and Loathing

COSMIC DARKNESS

If I were the sun

My consciousness would be its center

It lights the way to Earth, Mercury, and Mars

I see life dance on the light's edge

As it fades into Saturn, Pluto,

The moon and the stars

My darkness on the other side

I am tempted to take a quick peak

It touches my subconscious mind

My moral guide

I am less heavy here

Stronger, farther

Floating to the end of my solar system

Where the sun cannot reach

I wander

The barrier thin

I wonder

Who am I?

EMBER

It started out in an insignificant way

With a smiling gaze

Under a moonlit haze of night

He looked at me and said,

'Something isn't right'

My mind wandered in a maze

Hoping to find the right ways

To make him love me

But it wasn't love he wanted

He didn't like who he was

And therefore what he sees

The light in my eyes

The ease in my breath

He desired to be gone

Was I wrong?

Little by little

He put cracks into my mind

Every thought could not find

Its place

Until I became but an ember

Just so he could

Stay

QUICK DEATH

I want a quick death

Say the words

That will cut my breath

Tell me you don't want me

And my heart can

Stop beating

This torture

Wraps itself around my will

Suffocates and drowns me

My eyes on the clock

You don't stop begging

Let me die fast

Be done with it

Say goodbye

Bury me here

And give me

Back to myself

SIROCCO

Sadness swept across my soul

With the strength of the Sahara winds

I could do nothing

But hold my breath

Close my eyes

Wishing for a respite

From you

MELTEMI

I wish the might of the wind

Could carry from my heart

This dirty love

Take it to wherever she pleases

Take it away from me

Clear him from my consciousness

Let his scent evaporate

I want to be free

WISHING STAR

I used to wish upon all the stars

The moon

Wondering where you are

You told me you had one love

The love of your life

Wasn't me

I waited for the sky

To fall

To collapse

Like my heart, my mind

A thousand wishes lost to time

FELLED

I was not prepared

For the devastation

The infestation of you

A fallen giant

Made no sound

No one came to my rescue

I rot below the ground

My only friend,

The rain

And the morning dew

AWAITING

My heart died

A long time ago

Waiting for you to

Love me

Bury me

Here

SHATTER

You think you will fix broken people

But 'thank you'

Comes as a courtesy

Of

Breaking

You

Instead

SIREN CALL

Pull me down

With your sweet whispers

And hopeful eyes

Take me to the depths

Of your world

I hear you

Like a siren

A spark in me

A beacon to call

Into the darkness of the sea

Comforting like the night

Swallow me whole

I loved you so much

I did not care

Drown me

In disappointment

I lost my light

THE BLACK SEAS

I asked the sea to carry

My sadness away

Thoughts of you roll in

With the clouds

Your voice in my head

Heavy and loud

The sound of another life

In the distance

It can't drown you out

A cruel trick

The memory of you persists

Flooding my mind with

A thousand sleepless nights

LOVER'S DEATH

Burn my chest

I will never forget

The scars you've left me

In ruins

Words you speak

Have poisoned me

Death at my door

Knocking patiently

SWORDS

There's an ache

In my heart tonight

With our swords drawn

We want to win

Every battle

Every fight

What will it take

To end this emotional

War?

WAKE UP

I'm sleeping through life

Please tell me

When can I feel alive?

When can I wake up?

I am yours, you are mine

Reaching for the stars

For the moon

Reaching for what I cannot see

What I cannot find

Almost touching my dreams

Flying close to the sun

A chance to burn

I see the light far beyond

The midnight sky

Open your eyes!

I scream in my mind

Wake up!

Wake up!

Leave him behind

LOVE WAR

This love war

Ended not with a passionate death

But with many repetitive

Irritating breaths

So many useless

Careless fights

Where once you sounded

Like the light

Of twinkling stars

Words now so worthless

Like broken swords

My spirit awaiting for more

Every battle and every war

You lost

As I watched perched

From afar

What were we even

Fighting for?

CURSE

My ears burn tonight

Chest on fire

Why let loose words to cut

Breath caught in my throat

You are wicked

But don't know anything about

Curses

You will see

Words spoken to harm me

Will go back to thee

Times three

POISON

He tried to poison the well

Now that I'm not there

To hold his venom

He has poisoned himself

WELL

My mind goes into the well

Like a heavy rusted coin

Into the endless bottom

Is it worthless

Or does it still hold value?

Tossed in

Murky waters

Not shiny or new

No.

It holds

A wish

A prayer

Hope

Unspoken magic

SAFETY

I want to feel

Safe in desire

Even more than

Loved

DESTINY

WILDFIRE

Men seek to tame

Wild beasts and wild women

To stomp out their magic and their flame

To feel life in the balance

Controlled by their might

It energizes their mind and desires

But men can't control fire

When something burns

They are holding the torch

But by the heavens, women control the wild

They are the Force

THE OAK MOON

I've been told I'm like the moon

In the warm glow

I bathe you

You can see the way forward

The darkness of night parts way

Rocks turn to diamonds

Sand glistens like water

Silence kisses your ears

I encompass you

Always with you

When the dark side of the moon

Comes forward

The absence is cold

Unbearable

The darkness is so unkind

The sweet silence

Deafening

Unwanted

I am the same moon

WINTER

The mountains are for the heartbroken

The soul searcher

The never lonely surrounded by moody misty clouds

The quiet inner power of one, the singular spirit

The long crisp breaths

The brightly lit cold night skies

The smoky crackling fires

The romantic guitar licks

The wet snow dripped pines

The long nights with your thoughts and coffee

The brief white sky mornings with the birds

Solitude is heavy like the morning rolling fog

The clean smell of burning beeswax

The melody of a melancholy song

It's a deep chill down into my bones

I have myself

I am not alone

ORE

Every woman wants to be loved

She will trade her light

For a look

Sacrifice her will

For a lie

Once you wrestle and steal her heart away

She will be a version of herself

That neither one of you will like

She doesn't need to be tamed

Or calmed down

She doesn't need to be obedient

To be good

If you demand respect

By fear and force

You will never know the depths

Of all her hidden doors

And the love extracted

Will be as black and tough

As ore

PURPOSE

Every man is his own sun

How lonely to be one of only one

Surrounded by stars that are bright

But believing he is the source

Of light, of

Life.

Every sun begins fast with beauty

Not knowing when his last fire will be

His greatest feat and sole purpose

Is not to exist

But to die

And to die quick

KING

No man is my king

If men are kings then who am I?

Am I the king of my own domain?

This mind and body are mine

No man is my king

My mind and womb grows

The burden is mine to bear

And mine, alone

I create poetry, art, and beauty

I create life

The payment is pain

No man is my king

Let me receive knowledge

Fill the spaces of my mind with

Wisdom

Save my heart

To love myself because

I am worthy

Live in my body

As the blood runs

Through this ancient

Temple

I am

King

COURAGE

I deserve to be loved

With conviction and

Certainty

Don't be afraid

Jump in with all your might

And if you should fail

Climb out and try again

Or be cursed

With a life full of longing

And regret

Love me with a heart full of

Courage

Bravery

Gobble me up with

Unrelenting

Passion

Unwavering

Determination

Anything less

Is a love

I never want to meet

KNOTTED THREAD

I find myself counting the days

Where the fragments

Of who I once was

And who I am

Can correct its course

To meet who I will be

In a second

In a lifetime

I will find me

She is there waiting like

A knotted thread

Ready to be unbound

Time paused

But not lost

She will be found

THE MOON AND ME

She is never far from me

Through the lonely hours

She watches and sees

Every disappointment

And every flower

She pierces the darkness of my heart

And brings peace

And brightness

Never too far away

Or far apart

Guiding me

With her ancient wisdom

With sage advice

She does not abandon

Once, twice, or thrice

I feel her presence

She is my constance

Never alone

When she is at lunistice

My moon

I am home

WILLOW

What if my heart was never broken?

Would my spirit ever fly free?

Would my cage ever open?

Who would I be?

If fear won

And worry led the way

I would have never fallen

Never knowing

The ground was so close

Never learning

I could just stand up

The heart heals

Quick

The mind

Longer

But when it does

It heals

Much

Stronger

HIBISCUS

I found a piece of me

Floating

Between the heavens

And the sea

I plucked it from the clouds

Like a hibiscus flower

And let it reunite

With the other parts of

Me

THE SOUTH SEA

When you feel bound up

Look out to the sea

She will show you the endless sky

In her arms

A crest of kisses

From your future

A sight not yet seen

Make your wish

So that the wind

Will carry it to the heavens

And make it be

COMPASS

There was a dark cloud

A heavy foot

A generational curse

It stomped out my light

Stole me

Away from my destiny

I dimmed myself

For you

Sometimes not by choice

Most often

I allowed it

In the void

Unwilling to escape

There

The moon and stars

Lit the path out

Broke my curse

With my morality

My compass once lost

Remembered its route

GRATITUDE

Once the poison leaves

The blood is replaced

With gratitude

Hate unbinds itself

I am free

TREASURE

I searched the heavens

I searched the seas

For twenty years I was not free

I lost myself

In the shadows

I climbed the mountains and

The meadows

Unclear of where I was going

Or what was to follow

I surrendered my heart

With it my mind

I was buried beneath

The rubbles of time

I stood still and aside

So that you could grow

With confidence and pride

I lost myself some where

Some place

But today

I discovered my destiny

My fate

I was not gone

Just hidden

All along

Until it was safe again

To reappear

I was in fact harboring

The treasure

For all of these years

DAUGHTER OF THE MOON

I was searching for home

Guided by the stars

In the deep night sky

I thought I found it in you

My mother with me in her belly

Slept on the roof

With the moon watching over

At her zenith, I was born

Under her full moon sky

Between heaven and earth

Before the end of the month

I was flying under her ever present eye

I spent half my lifetime

In love with the idea of you

But it was her who guided me home

Under her magnificent light

From the start

I am a daughter of the moon

STAR SONG

I spent the day remembering my power

I spent the night bathed in my magic

My hair reaches for the wind

She whispers to me

The song of the stars

ACKNOWLEDGEMENT

To my readers, thank you for bringing me into your life. I hope you pick up this poetry book and sit by the fire or candlelight, take a sip of tea or whiskey, and let your emotions run free.

I would like to acknowledge my high school English teachers who first introduced me to Shakespeare, poetry, and literature. My love of writing persisted due to their early encouragement and influence. I am grateful for this gift of knowledge, passion, and perseverance.

My early memories of poetry and its inherent romance was shaped by Shakespeare's sonnets and plays, even more so with movies like *Shakespeare in Love* and *Ever After*. The Renaissance period has a special place in my heart. It was an era filled with fantasy, magic, romance, and celestial motifs- themes that lie at the foundation of my writing. Love poetry by Pablo Neruda, Rumi, and Cola Franzen's translation of *Poems of Andalusia* has greatly influenced my writing in this genre. I am thankful for their work.

I'd like to think of poetry as the sister to spells and songs. My poetry and writing style are very much inspired by songwriters like Taylor Swift, Lana Del Rey, and Stevie Nicks. The power in their music and lyrics transcends time and has continuously played in the background of my life. I often think of my poems as lyrics to songs that has not yet found its melody. I'd also like to thank writers like Alice Hoffman for creating the spellbinding world of the *Practical Magic* book series and movies. She has inspired me to add just a pinch of magic into everything I write.

To the strangers I've met throughout my life: Whether it was a serendipitous blip in time, a singular conversation, an inspirational story, a memory, a dream, or a wish shared in passing, I want to thank them for lending an ear, offering advice, sharing their life experiences, and showing softness and kindness to the younger me.

I've always imagined that the strangers we meet in this life show up when they are supposed to, guiding us like angels, into alignment.

ABOUT THE AUTHOR

Vanty is a poet and artist living in New York City. She holds a Bachelor's degree in Business Management from St. John's University and a Master's degree from Harvard University in Government with a certification in Social Justice. In this new season of life, Vanty has self-published her debut poetry book, *Desire & Its Impossibilities: Poems of Disappointment.* Vanty enjoys spending time in New England and the Catskill Mountains.

ABOUT THE BOOK

Desire & Its Impossibilities: Poems of Disappointment is an allegorical poetic story written over the course of twenty years that chronicles the stages and ultimate ending of a long enduring love affair. The collection of poems weave together celestial and natural symbolism with themes of love, magic, lust, despair, heartbreak, hope, self-worth, and rediscovery.

There are five chapters: *Desire, Devotion, Disappointment, Devastation,* and *Destiny.*

www.ingramcontent.com/pod-product-compliance
Lightning Source LLC
Chambersburg PA
CBHW020824150626
46554CB00018B/1882